I0422930

Fish
For Kids
Amazing Animal Books
For Young Readers

By Rachel Smith
Mendon Cottage Books

JD-Biz Publishing

All Rights Reserved.

No part of this publication may be reproduced in any form or by any means, including scanning, photocopying, or otherwise without prior written permission from JD-Biz Corp and http://AmazingAnimalBooks.com.
Copyright © 2015

All Images Licensed by Fotolia and 123RF

Read More Amazing Animal Books

Purchase at Amazon.com

Download Free Books!
http://MendonCottageBooks.com

Table of Contents

Introduction

The name 'fish' is a very broad term, meaning that it refers to many different types of animals, from sharks to goldfish to lungfish. Since there are more areas covered with water than there is dry land, fish are all around the world, and quite possibly outnumber most other animals.

In older times, a fish used to be anything that swam. A beaver was a fish, for instance, or a frog. Now, the definition is narrower, but still has many different creatures in it.

In this book, you'll read about fish and how they work, and then you'll read about different types of fish. However, since there are thousands upon thousands of different kinds of fish, it's really only scratching the surface of different fish species.

From the endangered coelacanth to the common goldfish, all fish are interesting in their own way.

.

What are fish?

Fish are animals with gills, heads, and no limbs with digits (like fingers). This includes a very wide group of fish, from sting rays to guppies. It even includes such large animals as the whale shark.

A whale shark.

There are four types of fish.

Jawless fish are a type of fish with no jaw; they are not closely related to each other. These fish include lampreys, which attach themselves to other fish to feed off them, or hagfish, which eat dead animals. It's not really sure whether or not they should really be considered fish, and there's a lot of debate between scientists about it.

Bony fish are fish with bones. This is the biggest group, including everything from clownfish to coelacanths. If a fish has a more typical fish shape (with fins, head, mouth, tail) then it probably belongs in this group.

However, there are other fish that fit that description: cartilaginous fish. Instead of having bones, these fish have cartilage, which is more flexible, or bendy, than bone. Sharks and sting rays are two of the members of this group. It also includes the whale shark, as pictured above.

Not everything that swims is a fish. Dolphins are mammals, not fish. They breathe air and nurse their young.

All in all, there are many different types of fish, and while one thing about fish may be true of most fish, there will always be some fish out there that defies the usual rules.

What do fish eat?

The diet of fish is as varied as most land animals.

A clownfish in an anemone.

One type of fish that eats other fish is the anglerfish. Instead of chasing down its prey, however, it lies in wait in the dark depths of the ocean, and uses its light to attract fish. It's an ambush predator.

The cookie cutter shark is another example of a fish that eats other fish; it takes out pieces of other fish with its lips and teeth, like a cookie cutter.

Some fish, however, don't eat other fish. Chinese algae eaters do as their name says: they eat algae. They are typically kept in aquariums to keep them clean.

Other fish eat insects and small animals. For instance, archerfish will shoot water at small animals and insects to make them fall into the water and then eats them.

Break down of food happens in the esophagus with fish, unlike humans where most break down happens in the mouth and stomach.

Fish diet is very varied, and it would take a very long time to list the way each one of them eat.

I like to eat a nicely grilled fish.

How do fish breathe?

Most fish breathe through gills; they have to breathe the oxygen in the water, so their gills don't work the same way as mammal lungs.

A goldfish; its gills are right behind its head.

A fish's gills work in this way: water is pulled in through the fish's mouth, and passes over the gills, which are a network of capillaries (small passageways). The capillaries allow the carbon dioxide, or the bad products of breathing, out, and exchanges them for oxygen, which is what a lot of organisms need to survive.

Some fish, however, can also breathe air. They gulp air and absorb oxygen through their digestive tracts (gut where the food gets absorbed). Others can absorb it through their skin. Some fish, such as the lungfish, will gulp air through their mouths and send it through their gills.

Fish and appearance

Fish come in all shapes and sizes.

A blowfish or puffer fish.

Most fish have scales. These are hard pieces that cover the skin of the fish, though sometimes it doesn't cover all the skin of the fish. Even sharks and sting rays have scales, though they are a different kind than most bony fish's scales.

Most fish also have tails. These are typically an end of the fish which is split into two fins, and they are used to move the fish along by swishing back and forth.

Fish also tend to have ears. These are on the sides of their head, and they don't have the same structure as human ears. Instead, these are protected against the water. They also have lateral lines, which run along their sides and up around their heads to sense things. This is done by hair cells (which are little sensors) picking up things like vibration in the water.

Some fish are poisonous to eat.

Most fish have eyes rather similar to other animals, though some more primitive fish only have eyespots. Most fish that are in the daylight (not the deep sea, where no light reaches, for example) have color vision, but not all do.

Fish also have swim bladders, which, while not visible, are very important. They are filled with gas, and they help keep the fish afloat through being lighter than the water outside. Not all fish have swim bladders, however.

Fish and each other

Some fish live in groups. These are known as schools, shoals, or aggregations.

A school of black jack fish.

An aggregation is a number of fish that happen to live in the same area. They don't really try to stay near each other, and they don't interact with each other in the same way as a school or a shoal.

A shoal is when a group of fish purposely stays together, but they are still independent; they look for their own food, they wander off a bit, but they always make sure to stay near enough to the group. They never truly separate if they can help it.

A school of fish, however, is a lot more organized. All the fish swim in the same direction and at the same speed, moving in a sort of cloud of fish. They are synchronized fish.

Fish generally mate by laying eggs and then having the male fertilize them. Some fish, however, carry the eggs, or even carry babies in a similar way to humans and other mammals. For an example of an unusual case, the sea horse male will carry the fertilized eggs in his pouch. He's not pregnant, it's just that sea horses rear babies differently than humans. It's sort of similar to a mother kangaroo; the babies develop and grow in the safety of a pouch.

What do fish do?

Fish are interesting creatures. What one does, another might not do at all. Here are a few of the behaviors (ways they act) of fish.

A pink kissing gourami.

Some types of fish are very territorial, such as the tiny damselfish. Others, such as large groupers, won't defend their territory, and will instead leave an aggressor alone.

Fish can actually make sounds. A human probably wouldn't be able to pick it up, but fish can do things like vibrate their swim bladder or grind their teeth together to either show their aggression, attract mates, socialize, or guard their territory.

Some fish live on the bottom of the ocean most of the day, like a flounder. Some never stop swimming, such as the tuna.

If a fish can't get enough oxygen in the water, it will come to the surface to try to breathe. This usually will happen in things like tanks and fish bowls, or if they're trapped in a small tide pool.

Sometimes, fish are just aggressive. If they're trapped in a tank, they will taunt and bite their tank mates; this is even more likely if they're smaller fish, like some gourami or cichlids.

Fish also excrete (send out of their bodies) ammonia instead of urinating (peeing) like we do. Our urine turns into ammonia over time, but fish's waste comes out as ammonia without that time.

Saltwater versus freshwater fish

Freshwater fish need scales that protect them from diffusion (meaning that the water pulls the salts out of the fish otherwise). Freshwater fish need all their scales, and if they lose too many, they will die.

Unlike saltwater fish, who have to worry about absorbing too much water, the freshwater fish has to worry about losing too much salt. This is because there is much less salt outside the fish, which means the water tries to move it out.

That's the largest difference between saltwater and freshwater fish, the last being better kidneys in the freshwater fish.

A lot of fish come up rivers to reproduce, and then pass away. Then the babies are born, and they eventually head back out the river to the ocean, where they live the rest of their lives until it's time to reproduce. These kinds of fish are called anadromous fish.

Saltwater fish are also typically bigger than freshwater fish because the ocean is bigger. Also, prey animals are bigger in the ocean, which means more food for other fish. Nothing in a freshwater lake could be quite the size of a whale shark, nor a great white shark either.

Sharks

Sharks are a cartilaginous type of fish. They have been around for millions of years, though the biggest species have died out.

Shark

Sharks have five to seven gill slits on either side of their head. They use these gills in the same way as most fish, with the water passing over them and the gills extracting the oxygen.

They also have rows of teeth; when some fall out, new ones move up. A shark can grow thousands of teeth in its lifetime, and lose just as many. However, not all sharks' teeth are sharp and serrated, because not all sharks eat large animals. Sharks that eat smaller fish have more needle-like teeth; sharks that eat things with shells have flat teeth.

Sharks' skeletons are made out of cartilage. This makes them much lighter than they would be if they had bones, which is important, because a shark must always move forwards. They can't go backwards or they die because they can't breathe.

A shark doesn't have a rib cage, so its mass (size and weight) is too much for it to handle being on land.

Sharks have eight fins, generally speaking.

They also don't have swim bladders, unlike most fish. Instead, they rely on a liver full of oil and their lighter skeleton to float.

Sharks hunt by using sensors that find the electromagnetic fields (it's like the energy that your body gives off) of other animals. This means they can sense other animals even when they can't see them. Their hearing is also excellent, as far as scientists can tell. They can hear other creatures from many miles away.

An interesting thing about sharks is that sometimes, on rare, rare occasions, a female shark will have a pup (a baby shark) without a father. This is called asexual reproduction.

Some shark mothers carry their babies in their eggs inside them, but other species of sharks lay their eggs. And yet more sharks carry their babies in a similar way to human mothers: with placentas and no eggs involved.

Most sharks eat meat, but some sharks, such as whale sharks, eat plankton, which are tiny organisms that live in the water.

Goldfish

Goldfish are the most common pet fish, and they are also the first kind of fish to be domesticated (made friendly to people, or able to be kept outside of its habitat).

Two red cap oranda goldfish

Goldfish are kept in many places throughout the world. They are freshwater fish, and have been the traditional pet of those who can't have furry animals for pets.

They were first made pets in China; this was over a thousand years ago. They are carps, originally native to East Asia but now spread to places like America, Australia, and Europe.

Goldfish can come in more colors than orange. They can also come in black, brown, white, yellow, and red, and in many different combinations.

They can't stop eating if food is before them. And they tend to eat shelled animals, insects, and plants, though they thrive quite well on commercial fish food.

There aren't goldfish in the wild; the closest relative that's wild is the Prussian carp, and that is a silvery color. The goldfish is a domestic animal, much like you wouldn't find wild Yorkie dogs or Dalmation dogs typically out in the wild.

Goldfish do not have three-second memories; in fact, they can learn to recognize different people. Their memories actually span about three months, and they can tell the difference between different colors and shapes.

Another interesting thing about goldfish is that they won't generally hurt each other. Some species of other fish will harm each other during mating season or because they want to protect their territory, but not goldfish. The only thing that can cause a problem is when there are faster goldfish that eat all the food during feeding time before the slower goldfish can get any.

Goldfish aren't always kept in aquariums; sometimes they are kept in ponds. So long as they aren't fancy fish, they are hardy enough to survive in ponds in good climates. For instance, Alaska would probably be a bad place to have a goldfish pond, but Florida would be a great place.

The problem with putting goldfish in a pond is that there might be too many, and that's not good for the goldfish or the other animals that live in the pond.

Marlins

Marlins are a type of perciform fish, which is a type that means that the fish are 'perch-like.' This means they have a particular shape, or similar build to perches.

A marlin

Marlins have a long spike in the front of their face; they also have a long dorsal fin, which stands up like a crest. They are very aggressive hunters, and can be many feet long. They are broadbill fish, like swordfish, their cousin.

They are very fast swimmers, faster than their cousins. Marlins were probably named for their bill ('sword'), which sailors thought resembled a marlinspike, which is a sailor's tool that was used with ropes.

There are a few kinds of marlin, and some of the bigger kinds are the Atlantic blue marlin and the black marlin; both of these types of fish are popular kinds of fish to try to catch by sportsmen.

Lungfish

Lungfish are so named because they have lungs. This is very unusual for fish; only lungfish are known to have actual lungs.

The lungfish has been around since early times, back when there were only a couple of continents known as supercontinents; that's millions upon millions of years ago. They have been more widely spread back then, but nowadays they live in the Africa, Australia, and South America.

Queensland Lungfish (Neoceratodus forsteri) in Suma Aqualife Park
This picture is from the Wikimedia Commons.

When drying out season happens to their habitat, lungfish simply and estivate (which is like hibernating for bears, but it's during arid or hot seasons). They can survive that way for months. Their metabolism (which is how fast they use calories) slows down a lot, and they are able to simply stay burrowed underground.

Lungfish have both gills and lungs, which means they can switch between the water and the air. This is done by readjusting the arteries and valves inside the fish, so that air can go in and out, and the water can go through. They are freshwater fish.

A Queensland lungfish is a living fossil, meaning that it hasn't changed in millions of years. When mammoths walked the earth, this fish looked exactly the same as it does now.

Lungfish are typically over 2 feet long, and by a lot. Only the smallest are 2 feet, the gilled African lungfish.

Mud skippers

Mud skippers are one interesting kind of fish. They are amphibious, which means they can live on land, including breathing on land.

A Thailand mud skipper.

Their fins allow them to move about on land; they skip forward, because their fins are so strong. They can even flip their bodies in the air.

Mud skippers live in land in tropical and subtropical areas (such as Thailand, China, Japan, and parts of Africa, as an example) where the water is drawn back in tides. This leaves the mud skipper out of the water during certain amounts of time, but they are well adapted to breathing air and moving about on the land.

They need to stay moist to breathe because they breathe through their skin and the lining of their mouth. They tend to hide when the tide is high, because they are in danger from other marine animals, such as larger fish.

They do all their interaction with each other on land, generally. They fight over territory, they mate, and they also do their hunting on land. Mud skippers eat small animals, such as crabs and other small marine animals, though they are opportunistic, meaning that they will eat almost any animal that they can.

Some fish become the dinner for other animals.

Coelacanths

Coelacanths are some of the oldest animals still around. They are more related to animals like lungfish and reptiles than more typical fish such as the goldfish.

A coelacanth fish

The fish is covered in scales that are like armor; they are nocturnal, meaning that they are awake and hunt at night. They don't typically move under their own power, but instead use currents and use their many fins to direct themselves.

A coelacanth doesn't have a swim bladder like most other fish; instead, they have a fatty lung that helps them float.

The interesting thing about the coelacanth is that it was thought to be extinct for millions of years up until recently. In the Western world (Europe and North America), the fish was studied as a fossil, while at the same time, the native peoples of the area around the Indian ocean had been fishing this animal for ages.

They are two types, the West Indian Ocean coelacanth and the Indonesian coelacanth, and both are endangered.

Coelacanth mothers don't lay their eggs like a lot of fish do; instead, they carry them around with them until they hatch.

Are you ready to go fishing?

Eating Fish

Your body needs to eat good food and fish are one of the best sources of protein and healthy things for your body. Fish feed families all over the world. The oceans and streams are full of fish to go and catch.

Fish found at the market are a very healthy dinner option.

One of my favorite things to do is to go fishing with my kids. We spend hours and hours out on the water fishing and having fun

Conclusion

Fish are some of the most diverse creatures on the planet. If we didn't have fish, we wouldn't have the same food source, pets, or interesting animals for our zoos. For that matter, fish are an important part of the ecosystem; if we keep their oceans clean, they help take care of us.

Pollution has caused a lot of problems for fish, as has overfishing; there are less fish nowadays in the world than there were one hundred years ago. It used to be that a person could catch a big fish easily; now, fishers are lucky to get smaller fish.

But fish are hardy creatures, and will survive. If fish have adapted to be able to breathe air and live where there is no light, then fish can adapt to anything.

Fish are some of the most beautiful and terrifying creatures in the ocean. From the gruesome angler fish to the pretty blue tang, fish are fascinating creatures.

Author Bio

Rachel Smith is a young author who enjoys animals. Her family had fish for about half of her childhood, including a large pink kissing gourami that liked to nibble at the other fish. Once, she had a rabbit who was very nervous. She's also had several pet mice, who were the funniest little animals to watch. She doesn't like dogs ever since a wild one bit her brother on the hand. She lives in Ohio with her family and writes in her spare time. She's also trained as a dental assistant.

Purchase at Amazon.com
Website http://AmazingAnimalBooks.com

Our books are available at

1. Amazon.com

2. Barnes and Noble

3. Itunes

4. Kobo

5. Smashwords

6. Google Play Books

Download Free Books!
http://MendonCottageBooks.com

Publisher

JD-Biz Corp

P O Box 374

Mendon, Utah 84325

http://www.jd-biz.com/

www.ingramcontent.com/pod-product-compliance
Lightning Source LLC
Chambersburg PA
CBHW050840290526
45792CB00001B/473